YOU CAN
BECOME
ALL FLAME

A Love Letter to an Actor

Bezalel Thatcher

ISBN-13: 979-8-9903612-1-8

Cover art by: Kylie Shea.
(www.facebook.com/kylie.shea.921677)

Printed in the United States of America

*My heart-felt thanks to Helen
for combing over it and proofing.*

"My brain ain't where the thoughts come from, it's where they go to die."
    –*From* Theo *by Paul Arendt*

An Introduction of Sorts

Beloved, you are amazing and lovable. I want you to know this, first of all, but I also want to be completely honest with you throughout this letter, beginning here. I don't know you as well as a person ordinarily should know another person when he is trying to make such bold affirmations, and there's also a bit of a sleight-of-hand here that needs to be dispelled: I know you're an amazing being and lovable, because I've met enough people to know that persons are amazing and lovable. However, I would also hasten to recoup, just as truthfully: from what very little I know of you (and it is very little, I assure you), you seem to be among the more delightfully amazing beings of these amazing beings. It was the part of you that you were trying to hide, no less, which tipped me off, the attempted concealment acting like an artistic relief against which your fervor glowed. And, furthermore, you are lovable because I love you. So, does that salvage the start here a bit? It manages to make it awkward for you, in any case. If you'll give me the chance, I'll explain everything. Don't worry: I'm very wordy and prone to plenty of prefatory descriptions.

Who am I? That's not as important to this letter as who you are, and in fact "who I am" might serve as a distraction to the matchmaking I'm attempting here. I'll reveal myself for who I am gradually through the song I'm about to sing. If it helps you to know on the front end of things, I'm a real person and not a narration device: a poet, primarily, and a novelist, a man, coming up on forty years of age. I'm as real as you're a really individual person (and not merely some fancifully-addressed, generic reader) whom I have in mind and heart right now. I want to sing a song of a love not to reveal myself – I'm just the messenger of this love – but because I want you to see this love and the invitation it provides for yourself, so that you can experience it for yourself in your own life. Essentially, I want to reveal myself here in and through and by my love for you, which you too can enjoy in your own way.

For now, as an initial disclaimer, let me simply say: this isn't romantic love that I have for you or that I want you to experience, in the sense of my desiring a romantic relationship with you or seeking in any way to establish such with you. There's no stranger's obsession or idealization to this love, though we are strangers. There will be no doorbells rung or your finding me hiding outside in any landscaping, and I'm also under no illusion that you're some immaculate angel who has floated down from the heavens. I do have sisters, I've known a lot of human beings in my lifetime, and (being a moderately shitty human being myself) I know better. Even further, if my intuitions and calculations are correct we will never meet one another. I've been wrong before (often), and I'm certainly not opposed to ever meeting you; it would be delightful to meet the actual person behind a brief mediation of a mystery, of course. I simply think it's beyond unlikely that we will ever meet. We don't run in anything approaching the same circles, and I have already poured out my life into something else which I love completely as well, something which demands quite a bit of attention and a getting "tied down" in one place. Anyway, I hope this disclaimer is enough at least to set you at ease that I'm not "hunting you down" in any way except in this admittedly ridiculous and indirect literary expression of the matter.

Nevertheless, the moment the word "love" and the phrase "I love you" get dropped onto the page of something like this, the author can't just presume they have an open and unobstructed audience with the other person. I would love nothing more than to simply and unendingly sing about my love for you and how you could experience this love, but that might not connect in any way meaningful to you or your life. That will have to wait until further on. Right now, this letter is a big surprise to you, and I must take into account whichever existential postal code you are currently inhabiting. If we knew each other or found ourselves somewhere together, I could probably convey it better and more quickly, but here we find ourselves in this absurd arrangement. I could say "I love pizza" and "I love my parents," and you could sort out the differences meant in the one ambiguous word, especially if I said it in-person. When an absolute stranger writes on an open page that he loves *you*, however, and you really do think it might mean *you*,

you would be right to become doubtful and to draw up your defenses. In fact, I'd be a little concerned over your sense of self-preservation if you weren't and didn't. I'm going to be singing about a particular kind of love while you and I and a lot of other people are floating around in a certain existential boat, a little boat which rarely if ever talks about the kind of love I have for you. It's not in our everyday vocabulary.

So, then, before I begin the song in earnest, let's meet in mind so that we can meet mystically in heart. Consider for a moment how we approach the messy business of our loves. It's in one of two ways, isn't it: either with categories or with pure circumstance. Most commonly, most of us waffle between these two ways of viewing love and cobble together something rough and workable for ourselves. But these two ways are quite often the only ways we know how to conceptualize what we experience as love, and those persons looking for a "third way" usually end up in one of these ways of loving or the other. Mysteriously, none of us loves in these ways, or (to put it a little less mysteriously) all of us smell a little bullshit in the notion of committing completely to one of these two ways of loving. So, well, many of us simply don't commit. It's why we waffle, in fact. It's to our credit.

One way of go about loving is to build and stick to tidy containers for love, those comforting and familiar categories. There's this container over here for "family," this one over here for "friends," and this one over here for "lovers." Most of us have a container for "adorable animals" as well, and some of us might find within ourselves the magnanimity to reserve a container for "acquaintances who aren't absolute evil incarnate." We shuffle people around in these containers from time to time, as emotion and circumstance dictate.

This way of loving tends to emphasize the intellect and to grow shy over emotion, and when we dedicate ourselves too rigorously to this way of love we get ourselves into all varieties of trouble. As Horace put it, you can drive out nature with a pitchfork, but she'll keep returning. When we become faithful container-dwellers, we begin to yearn for things we can't quite put an intellectual finger on, and in many cases we're simply miserable without realizing why. This is the eight-year-old version of us trying to name a "best friend" for the unofficial school census. This kind of love hasn't "filled out" yet, at best.

Case in point: there exists this mysterious little mechanism, perhaps a container to us, which we call "platonic love." For us, this is really just a plea to ourselves and to others to be allowed some more time. It's a holding cell in an attempt to quantify the indefinable. We most often use this little mechanism for people we would like to put in our "lovers" cat-egory, but we're currently awaiting some sign from these people to proceed in our campaign – a raised flag, an open door at last, a cracked window. Or, alternatively, we're the ones who've cracked the window or opened the door or raised the flag for the person in the "friend" category, in hopes of their agreeing to scoot their own butts over into our "lover" category, where we would prefer them to be. We keep waiting. In the meantime, we obstinately hug the containers to our heart and speak of "platonic love" to anyone who gets a little too close to those nerve endings, including ourselves. There are worse ways to live our lives, aren't there?

The other way of loving is to throw away all of the containers and to simply deal with individuals. Dedicated practitioners of this branch of the magic let the pieces fall wherever they may. A friend may morph into a lover and then back into a friend with with no "violation" felt or at least admitted, and an absolute stranger we meet smoking a cigarette in the alley behind the restaurant may be somebody we invite to bed tonight and tonight alone. There is no intellectual bullshitting about this approach in itself, and practitioners of this way can see right through the "platonic love" mechanism used by the people who are busy organizing the desks of their lives. We who've lived this out might make use of the terms that the category-dwellers demand, for our own campaigns of love, but we know these categories are rules in a game.

This non-category way of love tends to run with emotion and muzzle the intellect, at least so far as the categories go; there can still be quite a bit of rationalization, only we go about it unthinkingly. And yet, and yet – we who commit our lives to this way of love turn out the last light some nights, and in the darkness and the receding noise of the day we find ourselves (more often than we would prefer to admit) facing the terrors that lurk in our solitude, before we find relief from our consciousness in that night's sleep.

Have you ever experienced any of either world in your own loves, Beloved?

The vast majority of us try to ride through life with one foot planted in *each* way of loving, a peace treaty struck between mind and heart, because we intuitively recognize the need for both mind and heart in love and life. In my experience, most of us seem to secretly prefer to live among the containers for our own safety and general sanity, but we also seek the thrill and seeming authenticity that occasionally rears its rainbow-iridescent head in the stranger smoking in the alley behind the restaurant. It's good to stay alive as well as to feel alive. Given the chance, though, practically, most of us fall into one of these ways of loving as our default.

What is left unmentioned in all of this musing, what we've been inoculated against – what, in truth, is boxed up more readily by the free spirit than by the accountant of loves – is *actual* platonic love. We bristle. Isn't "platonic love," after all, a sterile, tidy, throw-away line that anal-retentive organizers like to splash around? Don't we resort to this sort of hedging when we're nursing a secret crush? or finding a crush from someone else to be a comforting and useful warmth? or when we're desperately trying to figure out how all these loves fit together in a workable way? "Platonic love" is an excuse and a means of self-deception, says the cynic within each of us.

What I will sing about in this love letter, Beloved, take it or leave it, is that we've bamboozled ourselves with all this referential bullshit. Our common use of something we call "platonic love" in order to play a game actually vaccinates us against the real thing. There is a love as passionate as that between any two lovers, a love as strong as any friendship, and a love as earthy as any family's – even making room for puppies and enemies – which grows under every love and fills out all our loves to their fullness. I would go so far as to claim that it's what gives the full earthiness, strength, and passion to all our other loves. I will even more absurdly claim that we all have the capacity for this strange love – I do, and you do, Beloved. We've found ourselves wounded and have clipped our own wings to avoid anymore pain, unaware we're denying our own capacity and need. We don't even have the equipment to begin understanding what this love really is, surrounded by the scant and haphazard tools lying all around this little boat of ours. Whether lost in our head or our heart or somewhere in-between, we're still limited to our own selves in our ways of loving.

To be clear, Beloved, I'm not and will never be some guru speaking down to you from a mountaintop. What very little I know of you would seem to indicate that you're a little cleverer than I am, and here I am writing about this shit to *you*. Receive it as a young child's crayon drawing, if you must: maybe not a Monet or a Matisse in oil, but crafted with deep love. Candidly, this whole subject is so profound as to remain beyond my expression even now, and (though I've set out boldly in writing this to you) I'm not altogether sure I'll be able to invite you into this love in a way that offers much persuasion. Until I first experienced it for myself, I would've been as skeptical as you probably are of this love's existence and its full expression. Still, "love is as stern as death," as the saying goes; I regret nothing in setting out to write this to you. Having experienced this love for myself and now having begun to love you, I'm compelled to share this with you, whatever may come of it. My hope isn't to convince "readers," because my own difficult experience in life indicates such an expectation simply isn't realistic. "Readers" are welcome to join us on this little ride, but this letter isn't for them. My hope, ultimately, is that *you* experience this love for yourself, one way or another.

Having Seen You

It was you, Beloved, who helped me discover the full dimensions of this love. Yes, *you*. I'd thought it was already living within me, and it was; but then you came along and shed light on the vast boundaries of it, beyond what I'd imagined possible. All the pieces were there. I'd read about this love in situations like mine, and people I admired had spelled it out. I was living in the midst of it, really, and had tasted it here and there without knowing what it was, should've felt it for *what* it was. I could've discovered the fullness of it for myself, theoretically, in some other way, but it was through falling in love with you that I discovered the immersive depth and breadth of this love behind all loves.

Here's how it happened. Every so often, I'll watch online videos about all sorts of things – history, life hacks, cat videos, comedian sketches, cooking, the usual. On a very few of these occasions, some suggested video or another will crop up in the side bar that I'll find intriguing enough to click on: some video featuring a person-of-note providing a demonstration or a celebrity being interviewed. Rarely, out of these few occasions, I'll develop a kind of intuition about that person.

Now, please forgive a bridge so soon in the song, but I feel like a defense has to be made here as well. I've brought my credentials into your court room, or at least my testimony about them, and I hope it becomes an amusing part of the song for you. According to the horoscope of our epoch, the Myers Briggs Type Indicator, I was (at time of testing) an INFJ: introverted, intuitive, feeling, judging. I didn't need a test result to inform me that I was intuitive and empathetic with a scientist somewhere in the mix, writing things down, but the testing confirmed my life experience of consistently hitting nails on the head by merely acting on a compiled gut feeling and my life experience of always yearning to help people. Additionally, when taking an IQ test, I "maxed out" (the psychologist's words) the pattern-recognition portion of the test. I don't know what this means precisely or how common that is, besides his running out of little cards with patterns on them, but all of this is meant to say: I'm not simply some weirdo who senses and speaks about vibrations in the world-soul of the universe. It seems to be much more down to earth: I'm a weirdo who often tends to have very good hunches about people for a number of somewhat quantifiable reasons, and one who then wants to do something about it (such as writing a love letter).

So, in those *rare* moments among the *very few* occasions in which I've clicked on a suggested video that pops up in the sidebar when I'm watching online videos, I've been struck by something about a person I see and think something like: "Hm. Something is going terribly wrong in this person's life in a way that is really calling out to my heart. I'll pray for them." And so I do; prayer is a fairly typical part of my life.

By "prayer," I do mean the regular, accessible sense we have of saying words to a deity, in this case a saying of words on behalf of these people. Also, for me in some cases, it means doing something especially and gratuitously kind or merciful for another person in my life, or else suffering something well and (in so doing) offering up whatever merits come from that for that person's good. If you wonder about any aspect of this concept of prayer, I'll explain it eventually. In any case, usually, I exhaust this impulse to pray for someone in that initial prayer itself after watching their Internet video, or I exhaust it over the course of a day or two, sometimes up to a week. It passes, and I get back to life's joys and demands and other prayers and pastimes.

Then came your video sometime at the end of 2023 or the blunt beginning of 2024. (I didn't mark it down in any calendar, and at the time I didn't realize how huge this event would be for me.) Your video itself may have been older, I don't know, and I don't have the willingness of heart to go watch it again. Okay, having shed my momentary cowardice over experiencing that video for a second time, I just now stopped writing, girded my emotions, and went looking for it on your channel. I couldn't find it; maybe you deleted it. Whatever the case, I've sauntered my way around the main point: I saw that video of yours at the end of 2023 or the very beginning of 2024. In response to your transmitted image, my heart immediately – immediately – went out to you, from the very first moments. This had never happened before, with the other videos. The sorrow behind your appearances otherwise came through instantly and raggedly, rending my heart. "Hm," I thought as usual. "Something is going terribly wrong in this person's life. I'll pray for her." So I did, as usual.

Beloved, this began a whole parade of events that I wasn't expecting. This experience of and response to your video involved much more than simple sadness or pity on your behalf: there's something unique about *you yourself* which managed to arc across the gap between who you really are on one side of things and my limited, mediated, two-dimensional glance at you on the other – profound depths of a personality, a surprising fragrance of a greatness-of-soul there that I perceived instantly but couldn't (and still can't) articulate – all of it coupled with your apparent sorrow in that recorded moment. It was the inner torture of perceiving a uniquely beautiful soul in this world who has been robbed of a happiness but is still trying her best to carry on. As busy as my life is, as full as my loves are, you stuck around in a new way strange to me, or (to return to my original imagery) my heart, having gone out to you, now remained trapped with you. I felt that sorrow, remembered that recorded moment of yours, carried that weight. As the months went on, I found myself praying more passionately for you, offering up more kind deeds and more of my sufferings on your behalf. I dedicated more and more of my free time to praying for you, and this continues to this day. This has all morphed from an initial empathy into a joyful hope, a fire. I carry you around with me throughout my crazy life and am happy to do so, in the hope that something of the prayer transmits.

What is it I pray for you? I prayed and pray that you find your ultimate fulfillment, the abiding joy that transcends emotions. Such fulfillment and joy would empower and console you more deeply than the good times and the bad, as it has done for me. To speak its mystery: you could become the fragrance that you are.

So, here I sit in my living room, waiting for a casserole to finish, writing this out, frustrated at the limits of language, and realizing how ridiculous it all could sound to you: one stranger praying for an almost total stranger, hoping for the ultimate fulfillment of someone whom he doesn't really know, writing to her now of a love beyond loves. For all I knew and know, whatever circumstances that prompted your face and posture to betray your sorrows have resolved themselves. That would bring me so much joy if true. Maybe I got some part of the intuition wrong; maybe you weren't in sorrow, or maybe it was just a bad day. I don't think so, in this case, but if so it wouldn't be the first time my intuitions have given me a false positive. If false, that would make me even more joyful than any sorrow's resolution. Maybe since recording that video you've found the ultimate fulfillment, the true joy, and I naturally wouldn't know (as we're strangers to one another). If you have, that would be the crown of joy for me. But I'll keep praying for you for, well, what looks to be the rest of my life. And it will be a joy and honor to do so. I'm sure it won't hurt, and I'm sure you wouldn't mind if you knew. Now that I've written it, I hope, somewhere in your own intuition, you *do* know of it and know it's for you.

As I've left us both anonymous, this idea of consolation is beyond absurd, but I somehow know that this will translate and transmit. I have hope and faith that it will. If someone else wants to think this is about them and they take my offered consolations wrongly, well, that's wonderful, too: collateral encouragement. Persons are amazing and lovable, as I said. But as for *you*: if you are ever in doubt that you are amazing and lovable, search for whatever hope might have transmitted. Remember the stranger who saw all of the first few seconds of a video of you, and saw your beautiful personhood and your sorrow behind the appearances you offered, and fell in love with you (of all the batshit-crazy things).

Seeing Another

Now, to be completely transparent, it began long before you, Beloved. There was a seedling before your blossom. You were the realization of how far this love can really go, which continues to this day, but it began with another person far more impressive than you or me. It began with a young woman by the name of Therese Martin, or (as she became called) Sister Therese of the Child Jesus. Most people know her as Saint Therese of Lisieux.

Saint Therese was the first person I'd ever read and thought to myself: "This is someone who thought as I think and felt as I feel." I'd never experienced this before. She was a very different person than I am (I'm a shit among shits), but seeing her was like seeing someone from across the room that you don't know do something you'd always considered your own idio-syncrasy. And, after that shallow and very self-interested introduction, then came the rest of who she was bashing down the barricades of my life unexpectedly. Her happenstance autobiography *Story of a Soul* changed everything for me.

In other words, she began the lesson that prepared me to love you, Beloved. Here was a woman, born in the cold of January 2nd, dead since 1897, for whom I felt an undying warmth of appreciation and a deep affection. She was so beautiful in her own unique way, even as there is a unique beauty in you (actual when I saw you, and potential). Her religious superior essentially commanded her to write an autobiography, which she found to be a silly assignment but obeyed, and later she was commanded to write about her particularly practical way of growing in holiness (her "little way"). Saint Therese wrote the last few pages of her manuscript in faint pencil, by the way (I've seen it with my own eyes), because she had grown too weak to dip the quill in the ink well. This twenty-four-year-old woman was dying of tuberculosis and writing the richest, most beautiful of love letters to her groom, full to the brim with suffering but also bedrock joy. She said that, when she got to heaven, she intended to spend that heaven doing good on earth. She burned as a bonfire of love itself. "When one loves," she wrote in one place, "one doesn't calculate."

So many chances to miss the sighting, Beloved! Saint Therese's superiors might not have commanded her to write her book – just as you might not have had the impulse to make that video, just as I might not have clicked on it – and she would have been lost to all sight. It would have been no loss to her, caught up as she was in joy, but I'm so thankful that she took the excruciating trouble to pick up the pencil in her obedience and finish her work. It gave me (and countless other people) the chance to fall in love with her.

In any case, after encountering her, I'd always intended to go visit her convent, where she's buried – to visit her herself – but it was a financial impossibility at the time. Maybe in twenty years, I said. Through some strange turns of event which aren't really pertinent to this letter to you, I suddenly found myself able to go visit her. I'd first encountered her through her writing in 2015, and right around the corner in the spring of 2019 I booked a trip with joy and set off to France.

I stayed in Paris for a day, I saw it, but I didn't have any eyes for Paris. Getting off the train in Lisieux in Normandy (have you been?), I instantly saw its beauty and that brought me joy, but I had no eyes for Lisieux itself in the moment. I walked from the train station, rolled my suitcase into the Tudor-looking hotel on one of the main roads through town, checked in, dropped off whatever I could as quickly as possible, and immediately went to the flower shop nearby, bought her a bouquet, and rocketed over to her convent.

It was a week in heaven for me. It was a week of love. Shall I try to describe the experience, out of my love for you? There was Mass at the basilica church built in her honor, a visit to her home and the church she attended, a brief visit to the museum, purchasing French copies of *Story of a Soul* and her poetry and lots of images of her for my house, and all the usual things alongside these (sleeping, eating). But I was floating like a third-party watching all of this other stuff happen. My memory of the place is how I spent most of it: rereading *Story of a Soul* on the steps of her tomb itself and praying. One night I awakened bolt upright. I felt a strong beckoning to go to the window, and looking out I saw the constellation Orion (from my vantage point) just over the rooftop opposite and directly above where she lay at her convent. In her childhood, as she recalls in her book, she'd felt that her name (the big "T" of Orion) had been written by God in the heavens. I'd already read past that part of the book and was presently absorbed in other things she'd written, but later it all came back to me. There were many other things besides this.

So, you see, in summary, you weren't my first. But this kind of love doesn't require "firsts." There isn't a competition to any finish line. There are other people besides you, within my reach, for whom this love burns as well. This kind of love can burn undying and spread to other candles, until one's heart – even the heart of a shit like me – can become a little grotto of presence and prayer. But that's putting it all backwards, at least in how I experience it. The grotto neither exists for me, nor is it a "place" I "go"; it just burns fervently there in my heart, and it propels me outward – to you in my prayer, for instance.

Anticipating a question you may have: why did I rocket myself to Lisieux to bring Saint Therese a bouquet of flowers, whereas in your case I broadcast a mere love letter and in the introduction speak of our never meeting? In the case of Saint Therese, I *knew* she understands this kind of love, because she lived it, wrote of it, inspired it, and sent out the summons. In her case, I was merely accepting her invitation. Meanwhile, this letter meant for you might someday sit in your hands (is, I hope, sitting there now), and that is enough for uninvited strangers to hope for, even those who are hopelessly in love. (I'll be offering you the summons eventually, but not to me.)

It should also be noted, with this kind of love, that you and Saint Therese bring something unique: yourselves. Neither she nor you fit a "template." You yourselves provoke my own unique love for each of you. One sister is a fire in heaven, getting things done, to whom I look up; and the other is almost certainly a shit like me, doing whatever good you're currently up to and on whose behalf (and in whose private honor) I can do a little good of my own, laterally. It all burns out of the same love, but it's two different persons and two different connections in love. You are lovable in yourself, and you have something to offer this world (in yourself) that St Therese and I do not.

Ecstasy

What I've come to realize in the guts is that this love as described isn't unique to Saint Therese or to me. We two may be the weirdos in all of this for our particular flavor of it, but all of us human beings have within us the capacity to love like she loved. In fact, I've found in personal experience (and that of my friends and acquaintances) that if we don't love in that capacity, things start going horribly wrong. And I think that's where a lot of things *have* gone wrong for those of us floating along in this little existential boat of ours.

How do I know that we all have the capacity and desire for this kind of love? I know because it's all around us; I have relationships, watch people, and have (and am dragged into) loads of conversations. I've seen this love's attainment and the failure to attain it in myself and others, fortunately and tragically in respective turns. Furthermore, the most diverse assortment of people have found it. The desire is there, within everyone I bump into or read of or witness, and out of the wildest corners of humanity its fulfillment flickers to life every so often. It greets us in the strangest places.

Let's begin with what we can both probably admit together.

The novelist Walker Percy wrote a funny little book called *Lost in the Cosmos: The Last Self-help Book.* In it, he explores the mystery of consciousness and the dilemmas in which we so often find ourselves. Among other things, he speaks of this bizarre urge we all seem to possess: the desire to transcend ourselves.

Everybody does it, even if they don't know it or articulate it as such. We're geared for it. Scientists do it with science. We artists do it with art. Many of us have done it with drugs or strange experiences. Even the attempt to deaden this impulse is the attempt itself: in that case, we seek a mere escape, but it's still an attempt. We sample a bit of all of it, in most cases. I write poetry and novels mainly, with some painting on the side. And you, Beloved, do it with acting (I presume acting is this for you), among what I would imagine are all sorts of other activities as well. We have all these helpful and funny names for these things we do, and yet we're all on the hunt for the same thing.

I haven't yet mentioned, by the way, that you are a truly amazing artist in your craft (the one that I've encountered of you), but it's worth saying: you are. I can confess this joyfully and freely without fear that you'll think I'm attempting to garner cheap rewards, because I'm not naming you or myself (beyond my pseudonym) here. I've dedicated one of my soon-to-be-published novels to Lynn Van Royen, who's a firecracker of an artist in her own right and who inspired the voice and conceptual bones of that particular story. However, I could have just as easily dedicated it to you on the same grounds. Van Royen painted a profound and moving story with her face in a few moments of absolute silence, and you did the same sort of amazing artistry in one of your roles that I happened to be fortunate enough to witness on the screen. It just so happened that, with the happenstance of my cinematic habits, I saw *Hotel Beau Séjour* before I saw three of the movies within which you worked your own magic. In these sorts of pitiful things, unfortunately, there is a "first"; you came in second, so you didn't get a book explicitly dedicated to you. Anyway, you're amazing at your art. You displayed a skill in your craft that was delightfully and subtly staggering – your subtlety was what staggered me – and it was a joy to watch you conjure the characters on the three instances I saw you at your craft. (Was your video on social media a fourth, I suppose?)

But back to the pursuit of transcendence: we all do something. Most of us do several somethings. And what are we doing, exactly, when we play the piano or dance to a song? We're ultimately looking for that experienced moment which T.S. Eliot describes in "The Dry Salvages" as "music heard so deeply / That it is not heard at all, but you are the music / While the music lasts." We're looking to transcend ourselves in other persons and in experiences, to become absorbed in something beautiful, to experience ecstasy (literally: "standing out of [ourselves]").

Percy describes these attempts at transcendence as rocket launches. These endeavors are gratifying flights which never achieve a lasting, stable orbit. Ecstasy doesn't last forever, after all: the music stops at some point, and the night eventually ends. We stand around expressing our joyful regret. As Percy hypothesizes, scientists tend toward a relatively shallow angle of launch at a fairly sustainable speed, so their orbit decays slowly and their reentry is gentle. Artists tend to have a rougher go of it; we tend to blast straight upward into the atmosphere as hard and as fast as we can to get maximum altitude, and then we come crashing back down in ballistic reentry with a violence equivalent to the transcendence. When many authors finish their *magnum opus*, they disappear – go on a week-long bender with drugs or bull-fighting or sex or all of the above. I wonder what it is you do when you finish work on one production. As best I can tell, most actors with a lot to offer and to experience try to muscle their way through publicity campaigns and "parachute" onto the next production rocket as soon as possible. That makes sense to me. But is the publicity campaign a joy for you, too? a victory lap, a share of the well-earned fun? or are such things a gauntlet for you, the closed tab for the transcendence? I wouldn't pretend to know. It's moments like these that make me wish we *would* meet someday, to hear your thoughts on this and your experience in this.

You see, it's not just shits like me and probably you, and it's not just saints like Saint Therese. Whatever our flavor of choice, we human beings just keep strapping ourselves to more rockets and doing it all over again. Why don't we ever attain a stable orbit and just circle our everyday lives in a state of ecstasy?

What I've become convinced of is that people like Saint Therese *did* achieve the most never-ending orbit that any of us can experience, but it's at a different angle and in a different way than we typically feel or think or speak. Her autobiography is saturated with this achievement. When I absorbed this reality, of course, I wanted to figure out what she was up to.

Purpose

What I've stumbled around, pieced together, received, and ended up with is one of the oldest, most well-known, and (for some) most boringly obvious of answers: our little artistic endeavors don't keep us in orbit, because while they can be a part of our ultimate purpose in life they aren't themselves the ultimate purpose.

You may agree from the get-go, Beloved, but these words also presume a whole lot. You might be asking as many of us have asked or do keep asking: Don't we all have different goals and purposes in life? hence why there's the dedicated scientist and the dedicated artist? Or you might be asking instead: Is it really truthful to speak of some "innate purpose," or isn't it rather more the truth of the matter that we find something within ourselves (or else don't) and forge a meaning out of this life we have (or else don't)?

I'm not attempting to hash out "star-aligned destiny" in regard to our professions of art, nor trying to figure out if I was predetermined to eat the breakfast I had this morning, or so on. I'm not speaking of cause-and-effect in the usual cold terms or in the intellectual terms of the objects lying in this boat and around which we can easily get our hands. I'm not even trying to get into classic anthropology in the classic way. Those are all fascinating and in some cases helpful discussions to have, things to talk about in the corner of a party that's begun to oxidize.

Burning love propels me onward to what I'm actually trying to express for you. I'm speaking of something that keeps popping up from *within* and *underneath* all the individual choices and circumstances.

The homeless woman, the teacher, the stay-at-home parent, the business executive, the young man playing the piano badly in the practice room at the university, the thespian, the girl with Down's Syndrome, the local Catholic priest, the human at the cash register at the fast food drive through, and the world-famous quantum physicist all have one thing in common: all yearn to transcend themselves in the same way. They yearn to transcend themselves in love. This has become, to put it bluntly, my cornerstone *cogito ergo sum* – "I think, therefore I am" – in regard to us human beings, though we could get witty and chisel it as *AMO ERGO SVM* (I love, therefore I am). We could find a myriad of other subjects on which to agree and disagree in regard to human life and human consciousness, but the fact remains: any assortment of human characters we could gather together and put on display before us would all desire a most central exchange. They desire to be loved completely and to be able to love completely. This isn't something I reasoned myself to, by the way, though reason was involved; it's something which hunted me down and swallowed me until I can no longer doubt it. The explosive force behind our rocket launches came looking for me.

The impassioned and growing artist so often

has the rewarding experience of making the art well, transcending high for a few moments, and then crashing to earth (perhaps parachuting onto the rocket of another launch pad, if lucky enough to do so). But I would say the artistic expression is as meaningful or as meaningless as the plenitude or lack of love within and behind it. I don't mean in regard to the art itself, which is a mysterious beast with its own considerations, but in regard to the fulfillment of artists themselves. The art may be good, but I'm looking around the canvas and easel at the artist.

In some cases, the artist has taken this most central impulse for love, this most central purpose to human life, and subjugated it to the artistic expression. Here is something, says the artist, that I know well and which I've found brings excitement, connection with other persons, the zest of living, an experience of raw fulfillment, even if just for a few moments. For the artist who mistakes this kind of artistic expression for ultimate purpose itself, things tend to end very badly. It's the difference between enjoying a cigarette with a friend *versus* only spending time with the friend in order to smoke more cigarettes. The friend, and not the cigarette by itself, provides what we're looking for at the bottom of every glass. On the other hand, for the artist who sees their artistic expression as one part of the whole pursuit of love, things tend to go quite a bit better.

There's been a hand raised in objection for a few paragraphs now, Beloved, and it might be yours.

The atheistic materialist would argue that love is simply a chemical reaction which our brains have evolved for themselves in order to encourage social bonding for the purposes of life and security. I wouldn't disagree that all forms of love are useful for such things and operate on that level, nor would I deny that there's a biological component and purpose to our loves; I wouldn't even denounce the atheistic materialist. However, I do *vehemently* denounce this cowardly treatment of the matter, if we simply leave it all there on the operating table and commence our celebrations over its supposed dead body. Anyone who has experienced romantic love can know that there's a little bit of the mating dance and sexual reproduction and two-pairs-of-biceps-being-stronger-than-one happening in such a situation, and yet the person who *really* falls into romantic love in a conscious way also knows in their guts that there's a bit more than just *that* going on as well. As I see it, it's better to leave those other parts (those twists and turns of consciousness) a riddle to be solved later or never, than to try to neuter the whole thing in such an abysmally asinine way.

Now, Beloved, I've landed here on something very unpopular, maybe even with you, something that I didn't find appealing when I first encountered it: the notion that there's such a thing as "human nature" of any kind. I've suggested we can speak about some kind of "purpose" common to all of us. Even going about it in the warm way I did is to imply that "certain rules apply," which gets us into the territory of an authority figure of some kind beginning to enforce rules upon all of us. Such an intellectual and imposed-from-the-outside concept – with all the dangerous consequences hanging over us – seems to threaten to squash our human individuality and the freedom of love. So I'll sing about that a little, if you'll indulge me. (Well, I suppose: if you won't indulge me, I'll find myself singing to myself. Here's hoping you'll indulge.)

Freedom

To the question of whether the stars aligned over your head this morning or merely your intelligence or your genetics aligned within yourself, Beloved, to impel you to eat a balanced breakfast this morning instead of a big bowl of sugar-laden cereal (or the other way around), I have no particular interest right now. That's as good a subject as any. I'm merely saying you shouldn't expect any musings on that from me in this letter, and my apologies if that's what you were looking for in a love letter. Pedantic warbling, anthropology, book references – *those* we expect in a love letter, after all, not words on destiny, right? I realize fully my own foolishness here. What I want to sing about forever is love, and yet for this moment (for love of you) that binds me to singing about freedom.

What does "freedom" mean to you, Beloved? How would you describe "freedom"? I suspect you would answer as we've all been conditioned to answer; after all, it's the air we breathe around here, the water we drink, on this little boat. Freedom is autonomy, of course. Freedom means having a range of diverse choices and no one there to compel us to choose one or the other. That's how we define freedom, typically.

Now, there's truth to this, especially regarding some of the extreme borders of the matter that we're trying to avoid by means of this philosophical creed. Our intentions are noble. Obviously, living one's life compelled at gunpoint isn't desirable or good; we all intuitively know this and rebel against the idea of the gun at our head. Being a well-actualized human being who can make one's own decisions is good. Perhaps the whole proposition of radical autonomy (not simply these defenses of the more obvious goods) sounds good to us, and many people seem to live their whole lives in that neighborhood. The trouble is that, if we buy radical autonomy's whole bill of goods as it's proposed every five minutes in our little boat, we learn the hard way that this is far too naive and open-ended for an actual human life. We end up living a kind of freedom which grows inward upon itself in various festering places. This kind of freedom threatens even the very good things we were setting out to defend in the first place.

I came to understand slowly – as you may have as well – that every choice connects to future choices and limits them, no matter what stories we try to tell ourselves to the contrary. Every choice we make sends us in a very definite direction, excluding other possibilities, in a way that is inescapable. We know this, too, in our guts, even if we don't admit it to ourselves consciously. We have a name for the anxiety contradicting our myth of radical autonomy – "FOMO," fear of missing out – when it comes to party invitations or dates. We're tempted to say "maybe" to every invitation, or we're tendered a "maybe" at the hands of others, because we all intuitively know that choices hold a determining power.

And saying "maybe" is itself a choice which excludes possibilities, though we don't tend to think of it in those terms. "Maybe" seems to us the obvious good, a deferring for the best option, and so we're often quite blind to what we're excluding by *that* choice. Ships pass each other in the night. It's ironic, Beloved, that, harboring such notions of radically autonomous freedom, this little existential boat in which we float remains full of people paralyzed, so often deciding not to decide until it's too late, and in many cases unable to make a decision even when the perfect moment to choose has arrived on an obvious parade float with signage indicating it as such.

There are the obvious cases which help us see the basic principles at work in the power of choice. Whether you subscribe to a certain philosophical or religious interpretation of the world, there are certain bedrock-solid walls into which all of us will run in our human behavior, from which we can't simply "exempt" ourselves through willpower. If you tell a big lie in a crucial moment, you may find some relief in that moment, but then a few hours afterward you'll find yourself dragged onto the stage to play the same part as before. In exercising your "freedom to lie," you have therefore chosen in advance to have no choice in the matter except to play the part exactly as before or else to come clean. With each lie added or elaborated, the chains of tedious fiction tighten. Now, if you tell the truth in that big moment, it will very often offer some suffering and embarrassment, but you also won't have to play a role false to yourself and to reality the next time you speak on whatever matter. You won't have to pretend and remember what you'd pretended. Either way, in regard to whatever choices we've made, we end up somewhere with them.

All I'm saying as a preface here, Beloved, is that choosing and even choosing not to choose means really choosing for something and excluding other things. That's simply how it works, whether or not we like it. Despite our initial distaste for this fact, we participate in it every day. Far from depressing or restricting, though, if we can assess the fiction about radical autonomy right-side-up and then sift it out, we recognize that the exclusion of things in choice also means that truly choosing something does actually *mean* something.

Choice isn't just about exclusion, after all, or even primarily about that. If I choose to have a conversation with this friend and not another in this moment, that means I'm giving the gift of myself to *this* person right now in a particular way. And that's meaningful. If someone chooses to marry *this* person and not the rest of the human race, that's a gift of self to *this* person. And so on. At the person's own wedding, they usually aren't thinking in any primary way "I'm so glad I excluded a whole bunch of good potential spouses"; they're thinking "I'm overjoyed to have given myself completely to *this* person and am overjoyed that this amazing person has given themselves completely to *me*." Sometimes we find some-one or something so good and so worthy of a love that, to enjoy them or it, we're overjoyed to say "no" to all the other options in order to give and receive a very good gift. You wouldn't, I think, and shouldn't accept a boyfriend's buying you an impersonal and generic gift for your anniversary that he has also meanwhile bought for everyone else in his life on that same day. You wouldn't, I think, be satisfied with yourself in giving *him* such a gift. Choice (and exclusion) makes these gifts meaningful.

Beloved, we yearn for a transcendence that can only be found, in a stable and sustaining way, in love. To truly love and to find the freedom to be found there, we must realize that we choose something (and things along that path) sooner or later. Such a proposition might at first seem restrictive – and in a secondary sense it *is* restrictive – but living with others and being able to live with ourselves means we must focus our efforts (excluding certain things) in order to hit a very good target. The one who truly begins to love no longer calculates whatever other losses.

Clipped Wings

Beloved, the strangest part of all of it (at least to me) is that I see genuine, authentic benevolence and an intuitive understanding of love all around me, all the time. Oh, yes, please understand, Beloved: this love letter to you is not meant at any point to be a mere pouting jeremiad "against" us, a "we live in a society" gripe. It isn't particular people with whom I'm angry at all, and I would distinguish the words being expressed from the people expressing them in most situations. Often, there's hardly a connection between the actions and the words. What absolutely pisses me off are the *words*, the ideas, that I've found myself expressing, that you've probably expressed, ideas expressed all around us and then echoed again and again, which march so many people into a retreat from the face of true love. There are the words that we broadcast, all of us parroting each other in a religious litany, and then meanwhile I see people (in all walks of life) up to all sorts of noble goods that run contrary – heretical and seditious – to the words we're always broadcasting. Maybe the difference between our actions and our words amounts to a simple cowardice to say what we actually feel or think. I know we fear consequences, and sometimes rightly so. Beyond that, I don't know for certain what's happening, and the ongoing divorce proceedings mystify me in equal parts confusion and hope.

Beloved, to hear ourselves in this existential

boat try to speak of "love" saddens me. I don't mean the meaningful, ordinary words of love we might someday speak to a lover in the bedroom before sleep. Rather, I mean the words when we feel we must posture in front of acquaintances at the dinner party. In what we express, we seem to have pieces of the picture – some pieces, maybe even all the pieces in some conversations – yet so often we have the whole thing jumbled up. I worry that we've spoken the jumbled-up words so many times at the dinner party that we've actually begun to believe them and to live them out. For true love to be something so vital to our existence and fulfillment, something we (to our credit) hold up as so important, our inability to converse about true love in any ultimately meaningful way breaks my heart. Has it ever broken your heart, Beloved?

Most of us speak of love as though it's summed up as an emotion within us. This is the most common way of speaking, and it's at the heart of much of our other talk. I don't know anyone who would deny that there's an emotional aspect to love, nor anyone who would deny that we find it easier to feel affection for certain people over others (and that that often means something profound). Nor would we find it easy to dig up someone who would deny that the experience of the emotion we call love is thrilling. All of that is so undeniable that I'll take it for granted. But our strange way of trying to sum up *all* love in the emotion itself turns the emotion into the blind litmus test of love, making our wills slave to whatever passion happens to roar through our hearts at any given moment. We should've wised up about this after our first serious romantic relationship fell apart.

If we're radically autonomous persons who can make any choice we desire to so make, moment to moment, and if we've fortified ourselves against any outside imposition while saluting every dictate of our emotions, then we have already abdicated our own souls and deprived ourselves of the possibility of true love. We've chosen to limit what we can do and be. You might feel an intense, warm, and intimate emotional experience of love for someone today, Beloved, but there's always the certainty that tomorrow or the next day or five years from now the tyrant known as circumstance will change and, with it, your "love" for this person (if our creed about love is true).

Thankfully, most of us don't abandon our parents or dump our significant others the very moment our passions shift. Most of us remain reasonable enough to not buy the dogma of love-is-an-emotion to *that* extent. However, to have this ridiculous notion of love clouding any part of our hearts is to risk depriving ourselves and others of true love. If we give ourselves to someone in what we would define as a complete way, and yet we're secretly holding in reserve some crucial part of ourselves that asserts we can act otherwise tomorrow, then we're telling a lie and will not enter into the abiding joy of the real thing. And even if we don't admit this is what we're doing, or even if we don't *agree* that it's what we're doing, we *know* this is what we're actually doing. We know our own dishonesty even if it's only a knowledge sitting deep within our bones.

What it comes down to is this: all of our predominant ways of speaking about love (in this little boat) amount to speaking in safe and guarded and timid ways, in ways that orbit around myself and that protect me. We cling to the one thing we can put in the test tube to some degree: the emotion. Even the boldest assertions of our loves, made with bluster, so often fall apart, and we sweep them under the rug of our hearts as though that will rid us of them. Our taught impulse in everything is to conserve ourselves, and we treat our emotions as though we must serve them, as though they are an immutable fact. This won't allow us to enter the true love for which our consciousnesses yearn in the same way that our bodies yearn for water.

Lest you be ready to raise objections here, I'll do so on your behalf: a good, hearty love of self is a part of love. I'll get to that eventually, Beloved. In case it needs saying, as a kind of disclaimer to keep your company: of course there's much more to love than what I've written to you so far. Emotions can tell us important things and guide us out of messes we otherwise don't detect. Also, our lives are messy; our hearts can be so bent out of shape that we only perceive our self-worth in others, and try to "give" ourselves "away" in a "complete way" that actually does us and therefore other persons very little good. Oftentimes as well, in our youth, we were more than ready to give love to a friend or a family member or a lover, and someone showed us how foolish that attempt was. The world has taught us many such excruciating lessons, hasn't it, Beloved? And most of us have taken each one to heart. In other words, I'm not attempting to drum up blame or shame upon you or anyone else for any of our participation in any of this bullshit we spout. That's not what this pondering is about, Beloved. We've come by most of this honestly, and unfortunately we give it out so often in the same way that we've received it.

What I'm attempting to say here, Beloved, is that we've been invited into games within ourselves and played them to the point that we no longer realize we're playing games. That's a tragic place to live. We, who pride ourselves on our autonomy, are slaves to philosophical bumper stickers that don't get us where we want to be, and we've become slaves to our own passions. There's this riddle that lingers within our own selves, a mystery in the sense of something tangible but (as of yet) unexplored. We sense nebulous fulfillment out there, and then we see love as we've been taught it through much abuse; and any road from one to the other is doubtful.

The Gift Half Understood

Our conversation in this little existential boat often (and sometimes without our realizing it) holds up romantic love as the highest sort of love, usually because it's in romantic love that we find a certain kind of personal intimacy and a wild kind of transcendence (a stepping out of ourselves, at least for a time). Some of us seek romantic love in order to sniff out another creature like ourselves. Sometimes the romantic love or the human creature seeks *us* out. Some of us seek romantic love simply for a thrilling experience or to deaden that annoyance of consciousness which plagues us. And so on, and often all of the above can be true throughout the varying seasons of our romantic relationships. There's a truth waiting for us here, which we sense innately.

Romantic love also appeals to us as the standard of love in our situation, it seems to me, because we portray it to ourselves and then buy it as we've sold it: as an exercise of that sacred autonomy we worship above all else. We take our autonomy as the first fact, and romantic love (as the definition of love) harmonizes with that autonomy more readily than the other loves in our lives. Setting out from this starting point, a person can easily begin to neglect the other loves in their lives as a "given" and regard the romantic love as something "more real" – as an accomplishment in autonomy. I get to decide who I'm "with," and I'm delighted to find that they, too, have chosen to be "with" me. That's awfully pleasant, of course, and there does exist a truth even here which helps us to ignore the shallow roots beneath this particular way of seeing things.

And all of this framing of romantic love is reinforced by other texture in our lives. We now hold the technological ability to immerse ourselves in constant sound and to absorb ourselves in visual distraction. I can choose my own adventure, and all I need is a streaming music service or a game on my phone. I insert input, and I receive gratification. Things which could (and often do) augment social connection also become for us – like merely bumping my genitals against other people – a mechanical way to verify my own existence and autonomy to myself. Romantic love easily serves a mechanical purpose alongside our other devices, in this mode of living one's life. And we discover it's more than easy to slip into this way of thinking and acting.

Beloved, let's begin somewhere else altogether. Let's say it's for shits and giggles, because it actually involved a lot of that. Let's begin with our birth – yours, mine, all of ours. Before we could really process what had happened, before we acquired the capacity to think as we're doing now, we found ourselves tossed into the middle of a rather preposterous situation. Two lumbering, tired, improbable creatures are lugging us around everywhere. We become familiar with the fragrance and texture of a certain blanket without realizing what familiarity is. (I was the oldest of my siblings, so that's how it was for me; for you, as I understand it, there were a couple of other little human beings who came along before you did – strange, smaller versions of the lumbering parent creatures, darting around and not necessarily knowing how to hold you.) If things go more or less how we all recognize they're supposed to go, we're hearing mostly comforting voices and receiving nourishment like a little sack of potatoes, receiving and receiving. We offer some transcendent and instinctive joy, perhaps, but mostly (so far) we have contributed morning sickness and a ridiculous amount of labor pain to our mothers, among all sorts of other burdens, now followed by our bodily waste and crying in the early hours of the morning.

This is where you and I and all of us began. So far as we can tell, we chose neither to come into existence nor when or where we were born, and yet here we are now, decades later. Four human beings pursuing their own life or lives, expecting or not expecting us, gave you and me our unique shapes, Beloved. Hopefully, for you as it was for me, your parents cared for you as best they knew how, before you could really contribute anything quantifiable or publicly noteworthy. For all of my accomplishments in life and all of yours, we both sit here not only as the authors of so much but primarily as recipients of all of it through the gift of our existence. Both you and I are gifts given to ourselves as much as we are to the human race. We speak so often of our "existence," but really we *sub*sist as a gift.

Our beginning reveals something about us which remains true. If you or I have become the masters of our respective domains and of our own destinies, nevertheless: we didn't conceive or give birth to ourselves. However we desire to look at the matter, the fact remains that there was a time when we didn't exist, and then suddenly we *received* existence. Everything, for us, begins in a gift which persists even now.

It's a queasy business to admit a loss of absolute autonomy, but our being given existence also tells us a lot about what will bring us fulfillment. Much has changed, but who we were is who we still are. We are strange beings brought into existence who, even in the potato-sack phase, learned the language of gift. After the potato-sack phase – namely, as soon as we could crawl or waddle around enough to do so – we began furiously giving gifts and tokens of love and gratitude to other people. Whatever you want to call it, Beloved, we are gifts to ourselves, gift-receivers, and then gift-givers. And, at the end of the day, we want to give ourselves back. That's what all the gifts are about. This is the starting place, a truth that runs deeper than even our desire for autonomy.

It isn't all so bad to face this truth, and it will end up better than we imagined it could. We want to delight in the gift of others, and we want to give ourselves in the little, ordinary, everyday movements – to family and friends and even acquaintances – as well as to someone special in a romantic way and/or to worthwhile causes. We want to be delighted in love and to be a delight in love. You and I and many others are already doing it, and we all know at least a little something about it. It's better to simply admit it to ourselves all the way instead of continuing to stew in our own fears and getting it all confused and backwards.

Liberation

After all the wading, we can finally begin to get to a fun part of the song, Beloved, and I can sing this from my own experience.

True love often involves the emotion we call love and, in fact, usually involves emotions of some kind or another, because we're vibrantly emotional creatures. In other words, true love is never boring. However, true love also manages to transcend all of the movements of our heart, helps direct and channel them, because it's rooted in something deeper than those movements. True love involves choice, not in the sense of "expressing my autonomy" or anything else as flat and sterile and self-referential as that, but rather the choice of commitment that comes from self-knowledge and discipline. I choose this good beyond myself, and I choose this as strongly and as freely as I can. When we're doing things right, we choose the best things permanently. The perfection of true love is being able to fully receive other selves and to fully give ourselves.

This kind of love elevates us beyond our usual slavery to circumstance, because I can commit to someone within myself and stay true to this, no matter if even I myself find my heart changing five minutes from now. And when we do this, if we learn to choose well, the commitment itself brings a stabilization and joy that goes beyond whatever I'm feeling emotionally at any particular moment. I am free to enjoy great things in a consistent, purposeful way because I've concentrated my efforts and restrained myself in certain things. The gift-giving becomes good and better. For all the bundle of mystery that love is, at its core it's an act of the will; true love is a "yes" that continues saying "yes" as life and the "yes" itself unfold.

This mystery is found (hypothetically) in the marriage commitment we human beings make with each other, of course, but it can run across the entire board. In something approaching an ideal life, we experience the gift of selves within our families – our parents, our siblings, our grandparents – and then begin reciprocating our own selves back to these people. With friends, we tend to stumble into a lot of people, have affection for some of them, and then commit ourselves to them.

With a life falling far short of the ideal, in which many of us have found ourselves, persons whom we love do burn bridges in choices completely beyond our control, and it's quite natural for us to experience all sorts of emotions over this. Yet if our commitment is strong enough we can still love these people, even if liking them or having a particularly close relationship with them is simply impossible or unwise. We can will their good and (if our lives intersect anything to do with these people) act in harmony with their well-being.

That's true love in a very messy world, and it doesn't always mean our emotions go along with us in this, at least at first. If someone's parents were abusive to them as a child, true love for the parents usually doesn't involve a warm, intimate relationship, but there can still be a willed, general concern for their good on the most basic level. If a friend betrays someone, this will almost certainly alter the path of the friendship if not end it, but the betrayed is still free to love the betrayer, even in distancing themselves from the betrayer in anger and sorrow.

Where does this whole process of love begin for us? Does it begin with an emotion or with the commitment? Sometimes it seems to begin in one place, and sometimes in another. If you meet someone who stirs up your emotions in a desirable way, you might find yourself ready to commit to this person quickly and with great agility. This is the way we're most accustomed to experiencing it. If you and another person find yourselves on a sinking ship and you don't particularly like each other, you can still commit to the other's good and find love in this even if, at the end of the day, you still don't like each other. But, then again, you may end up liking one another because of the love manifested in the shared experience.

Where does love begin, emotion or commitment? That's a question I've often wondered, usually in the aftermath of a failure on my part or that of another person, but now I think there's a different and better answer. Love begins neither in the emotions nor the commitment but in the *encounter* with a person. From there, true love will typically involve a lot of emotion – which can help us be good at true love – and *always* involve commitment. Emotions are good and can often move us (more easily than otherwise) to do what we should be doing, and yet at the heart of it all is the encounter with the person themselves and our ability to commit. Sooner or later, we must commit if we're going to give the gift of ourselves in a complete way that brings us and others joy and fulfillment.

Am I trying to put restrictions upon you, Beloved, or box you in with words? Have we gone too far? The approach to love as commitment of self becomes a liberation. I suspect, Beloved, you understand this whole thing intuitively. This is what we artists do every day of our lives, in a different way. Commitment is a human experience, but we artists (of all people) should certainly understand this in our gut. It's what some artists' family members or friends have said at various points along the way: that the artist has gone "too far," that they've committed themselves to an endeavor "too deeply." So, most of us artists have already "bought in" on the artistic side. Why not wonder if this is a little glimpse of love itself and weigh the wager there?

When the Sex Becomes Tedious

When I'm writing a poem or a novel, Beloved, there are all the thrilling emotions that draw me in and tangle me into the work itself; there's the joy of practiced, skilled creation and the pouring out of felt thoughts and solid characters and turns of phrase and a striking world. On the rare occasion that I get the chance to collaborate with a writer I respect, it's an experience like no other. And sometimes I stay up too late writing and pay for it in the morning. All of it is the thrill of flirtation, it's infatuation, it's teenage love, it's addictive, it's natural, it's all good so far as it goes. Eventually, though, this ride fades away in each project, at least for awhile.

In poetry, after years of working at that beautiful craft, the disappointment always comes with the finishing of the poem and the reception of it. Sometimes I see that I've struck upon the truth well (and the beauty in the truth), and the disappointment comes in knowing that I will never be able to experience stumbling upon those exact words in that arrangement ever again. More often, poetry disappoints because I *see* what I was trying to express, and the finished work falls far short of the thing itself. Maybe I've done well, but the artifice fell short of the actual. And then, after the poem is received by someone and that moment dies, there's the enriched emptiness of completion.

When it comes to writing novels, I let a first

draft "rest" for at least a month before getting back to it, during which time I can very easily experience anxiety or boredom in leisure if I don't jump into something else. Mind you, this runs in the background while my life roars on with other loves and completions. It's a strange experience. And then any thrill that remains for any novel vanishes when I go into the second-draft editing and receive the bad news from the editors and then stumble upon beta readers too busy to help me. Abruptly, money involves itself. Often, after finishing a novel, I can't stand to look at it for quite awhile, despite being greatly pleased with it.

Supposedly, I began dabbling in the art of writing at the age of ten because it's a means of expression that's intoxicating, exciting, and empowering. Supposedly that's why. Yes, that's there, I suppose, but what are we to say of all the frustrations and boredom and disappointments in a life already full of such things? Mavis Gallant once described writing as a love affair, namely in that "the beginning is the best part." So why do writers keep chasing this shit all the way to the miserable end, then? Is it just Percy's theory about the thrill of the rocket launch, the rush of leaving the atmosphere, seeking a higher altitude? Is that enough to keep the whole thing rolling?

Behind the rocket launch, there's something else, too, I think. Crafting art is truly intoxicating – intoxicating enough to get addictive – but those of us who've ridden that rocket enough and who've gotten better at it recognize something deeper always threatening to sweep us away as well. Even the sadness and boredom and disappointment and anger become worth it, somehow, even when everything comes to naught. Those short stories over here which frankly suck or those novels over there that will never see the light of day, at least so long as I'm drawing breath – all of those miserably failed attempts – are somehow worth it. They're worth it even if they're so terrible that another work can't cannibalize even the smallest bits of them for a better story, even if I can't put them to any other use right now. We writers tell ourselves the losses make us better writers, and maybe they do sometimes. Some of my own writing has made me a worse writer, dragging me through wildernesses until the funk breaks and I can recuperate. Still, sooner or later, a writer will realize that there are easier ways to feel expressed and rewarded, and we continue writing. We try our hand at expressing and contributing something else and even win the occasional admiration and praise and appreciation, and yet we continue writing. I continue writing, even having "obtained" rich loves and various means of fulfillment in other ways; saying I "enjoy" writing is oversimplified and overstated, but here I am, still writing.

I wouldn't at all presume to speak of your experience of your artistic expression, but I suspect some of my experience collides with some of yours, as

I have artist friends in other branches who've shared similar impressions as those I've expressed to you here. Admittedly, we writers are a weird bunch in the family tree. Our own consciousness channels the electrical current of creation with no other medium between the idea and the art itself, as Walker Percy noticed. Collaborations help, if we can muster up the trust to show our "children" to other people. All granted, but *some* of my own experience seems to harmonize with the other expressions of art.

All of the ups and downs I've described in writing run analogous to any human relationship, most notably with siblings and with lovers. Beloved, why do we keep putting up with these shits? Why do *they* keep putting up with the shits that *we* are? Sometimes it's social norms and a pride to keep up appearances, sometimes it's whatever you want to call it – a mere biological instinct or natural bonding or what-have-you – but at the end of the day we are flabbergasted and admit that we love these people. It may be oversimplifying or overstating it to say we "like" this one, or any of them all the time, but even in the midst of the fight we do care deeply for them (hence the fight). In some poignant glimpses of the love behind all loves, we realize we would probably die for these people if pressed to it. We have this sneaking, gut-wrenching feeling that it's true.

I began this letter, Beloved, speaking of "platonic love." It's what burns within me for you, and I want to assure you that I'll have it for you no matter where you go in life or what you do. As I said at the beginning as well, I'm sharing this with you in the hopes that, if you haven't experienced its fulfillment yet, you will. Of all the loves we can have, which are all good in themselves so far as they go, this love is the most misunderstood (in my experience) and it's the one that fills out all the others. Once we participate in this "platonic love" in earnest, we find all our other loves making more sense and becoming more "themselves." I think we could say this love is the love that makes all the other loves eventually and enduringly possible, when the last word is said. We're aware of erotic love, of course, and the love we share with friends, and the love of parents for children. Most people who write about these things presume these loves are distinct, and I'll take it for granted in order to move on to the greater thing. What I dubbed "platonic love" earlier – mainly borrowing this term from the people who prefer to categorize things – is something else besides these other loves, and we could also call it by the Greek word *agápē*.

Now, I've heard people call this kind of love a "love of mankind." Sure, that description works to a degree, Beloved. That's a little cheap and timid for the actual experience of it. Yes, it's a general benevolence and goodwill, but it's a love willing to do anything for the good of another, a sacrificial love, a love that gives even without any expectation of reciprocation. As I've experienced it, yes, it's a general benevolence. It's hardly bland or abstract, however: it goes specific and becomes absolutely and utterly passionate. It endures all things and becomes a glowing furnace within your heart that simply won't go away. It empowers every other kind of love it touches within our hearts.

There exists an analogue to erotic love in the crafting of art, and we all know about that. Art gets compared to making love for obvious reasons. Well, what of the artist who keeps making art when the "sex" gets bad or there's no longer any enjoyment? Why, on those bad days when we don't desire the artistic expression, do some of us simply continue doing it? There are a lot of possible reasons. I think one of them which only just manages to escape our notice, almost always – and goes deeper than the em-powerment of self-expression – is the joy itself of abandoning ourselves to the being emptied. This joy points to something bigger and more integral than just artistic expression, meant to be part of every-thing we do: a true love.

If you and I want to call this love "platonic love" here and if we can also manage to escape the gravitational pull of the passionless connotations that we've imported into it, that's fine. It's easier than importing Greek words into the conversation. However, this love is anything except placid and dead. Being consumed by this love brings about our birth into who we are meant to be.

Self-interest and Empowerment

I'll keep trying to make this work, Beloved, but I'm pondering the road traveled and the road ahead and don't think a love letter will suffice for all this. This is a monologue by its nature, and (as this drags on longer and longer, with all my hemming and hawing) the potential for it all to come across as "mansplaining" builds. I well know, Beloved, that you may be miles ahead of me on all this, several chapters ahead. Yet I don't want to presume anything in regard to something I feel so deeply and know to be so important. I have no idea where you actually are out there, where this will intersect you. I have an intuition, and that's merely more dangerous.

We were made for sacrificial love, I've proclaimed, and this love is at the heart of all our loves and fills them out. You may have no objections to any of this, Beloved, but I had plenty of objections to the dangerous edges of *all* of it when first confronted with this pitch. It sounded to me almost correct, with strange dangers on every border.

How is such a notion of "true love," as I've described it, not actually dangerous to the person who channels it? Isn't this a good way to end up a perpetual door mat, abused and manipulated? Also, how is this notion of love not ultimately selfish and naively delusional? This love is just me pouring myself out, supposedly, and it doesn't even matter if it's requited. In other words, this could seem to border on or cross over into a delusional inner dialogue. This could seem like another flavor of the same insufficiency I was lamenting earlier, a different kind of self-absorption that lacks true connection with other persons.

First of all, Beloved, self-absorption and selfishness are radically different from self-interest. We hear people conflate the two all the time all around us, even to the point of excusing bouts of selfishness. Selfishness is a degradation of self-interest, just as lust is a degradation of healthy erotic fulfillment. Selfishness is seeing myself – in one action or in habituated actions that become an entire lifestyle – as the center of the universe, thinking of whatever I desire as mine by right (something due to me) simply because I want it, and then demanding it as such, even if it's not actually mine to demand. Self-interest is recognizing that I'm a person with certain rights in harmony with a community of persons, a person with intrinsic dignity, and a person with the power of a will of my own. Selfishness goes against who we are as gifts and gift-receivers and gift-givers, whereas self-interest is a just and good recognition of who we are, what we can expect to depend on from others, and what we have to offer others.

The love behind all loves as I've described it, Beloved, harmonizes with self-interest. You and I were made to give ourselves as gifts, and when we don't do this well, it actually hurts us – if not with immediately obvious effect, then in the longer theme.

It's within my self-interest, ultimately, to give myself away as a gift to other people. Ideally, this gift is received well and this provides joy to other people – I'm not the center of the universe or the love itself – but even if this gift is rejected and the joy doesn't transmit, it's within my self-interest to offer it anyway. While this love is other-oriented, it's *my* participation in this love, and it's within my self-interest to offer it.

And, second, Beloved, this posture and giving of the gift of self isn't something given in a delusional vacuum separated from all context. We need to learn to be powerful and intelligent creatures in order to really know how to give such a gift well and then to go about doing so. I'm not writing to the battered spouse, saying they should just "stick it out" and "behave" as though all is well. In the more horrific of these situations, the prudent person needs to protect the good that is themselves by removing themselves from the immediate threat; such would be as much a gift to the violator who is giving the terrible gifts as it is to the victim being abused. Both the violated and violator are injured by the violator's violation, in dif-ferent ways, and it's often the case that part of the gift of the violated to the violator is to prevent the violator from further violation. And the person who can, in their self-interest, discern this as part of the gift given is a powerful and intelligent creature who can nevertheless give the gift of self in all its possible expressions without lowering themselves to the terrible gifts of the violator. (In any case, as an aside, I of course hope none of this describes any situation in which you've found yourself.)

This love behind loves presumes, is really only capable of being expressed, if we understand the nature of the gift and how to give any gift. We've spent our whole lives learning this in the small expressions, and it's the same for the largest gift we can give. We, in fact, usually give ourselves most largely and fully in the habituated small gifts. Giving "big gifts" is difficult if not impossible if we don't know how to give the everyday small gifts of self. This love isn't playing games within our own minds or "being nice" or any other slogan we can cook up. You and I are gifts and gift-givers at our core, and our default posture is meant to be one of giving ourselves to others; and then we only get good at it by *doing* so. How we give ourselves will look different with an acquaintance, with a lover, with an enemy, and so on, depending on what we discern would actually be a gift and what we discern the gift-receiver is capable of receiving. There's ongoing learning to this.

Now, it's one thing to give good practical advice or assistance to someone beleaguered and suffering ongoing injury at the hands of another, and it's quite another thing to camouflage our own timidity, riding on those anecdotal coat tails in every circumstance. There has been far too much of our warbling about our own self-interest and self-worth, by which we so often mean mere competitive selfishness, and meanwhile we seem to have forgotten our own gift and the need to give it. For all the debates about ancillary issues which have their own importance – political, philosophical, moral – the central cataclysm to our life in this little existential boat right now is the way in which we can't love to our full capacity and have even stripped out the capacity to speak about this lack. We're too busy speaking about and asserting our wills against other wills and making sure we don't end up the violated, even if (by pushing so hard) we end up becoming the violator accidentally.

Sincerely, Beloved, this is why I've grown tired of our usual words on "empowerment" with which we busy ourselves so often. True empowerment is something worth talking about, but we are usually content to parrot catchphrases in an imitation of the people living with the real thing, in our groping around in the dark for what we mean to mean. The dogmatic assertion (even to my own detriment) about my radical autonomy, and my vigilance over this sacred assertion – all of it is a fear response. That's what's going on. That's it. It's a reaction and a counter-assertion, a pushing outward to arm's length, and that's all. In other words: the original violation imposing itself upon me, to which I'm reacting, still has absolute power over me. If I continue down this way of existence, I can easily become defined by mere rejection. What would it be like, Beloved, for us to be truly empowered enough to find ourselves freed from a cycle of mere, perpetual reaction? What would it be like to grow beyond an amoeba merely responding to stimuli?

At our dinner parties, we often conclude the assessment of things by describing empowerment in terms of a driven, courageous person who overcomes discrimination and oppression to accomplish a major life goal of theirs. That's all good, all things being equal, but this person might be empowered in the way that really matters or might *not* be empowered in the way that really matters. We've stopped the train outside the station and disembarked already. I would rather cut through the secondary indicators, the popular and safe indicators, remove any distracting and dishonest bullshit from the picture, and sing to a different tune. If we're going to attempt a portrait of empowerment, I want to sing about (say) the abused spouse who knows how to establish good and strong boundaries with the abusive spouse and in the aftermath still manages to raise their kids the best they can, and who is still capable of all kinds of love through it all, dying to selfishness and pouring themselves out and receiving the gift of every fortunate circumstance and personal will as an enrichment, and harnessing every unfortunate circumstance and personal will hurled at them as further momentum. Such a person is truly free. Such a person is a force to be reckoned with. That's a fully empowered and empowering person.

The secret to the true love at the heart of all loves is being willing and able to die from it and still live and persist through it all, taking circumstance into account prudently but being unhindered by fear and mere reaction.

Having a Stomach

Beloved, I remember eons ago hearing Billy Joel's *Only the Good Die Young* for the first time and, even with my being quite vibrantly opposed to the Catholic Church and that vision of life, thinking: "Hm, I don't know about all that." A gigantic institution that's somehow managed to survive two thousand years of cataclysm, external persecutors, and its own diabolical and stupid and incompetent personalities from within, has apparently failed to "count on" the narrator circa 1977, huh? That's a miraculous lapse.

Now I know how to better articulate my agnosticism, and for you, here: the true saint has more in common with Billy Joel's narrator than at least the narrator realizes. (Billy might have known and just found the lyric to be too good a depiction of a character and a story to resist. I would get it, and I won't presume. Or else he has figured it out by this late hour, for all I know.)

Yes, the true saint is like the narrator in that song. To be clear, Beloved, by "saint" I'm not talking about the person who is generally good or "nice" (our little existential boat's way of fumbling around at the mystery) and yet who's caught up deeply in the same games the rest of us tend to get caught in: that is, the person who has simply chosen the hobby of devout piety and moral rectitude as a cover story for their personal appetites and endeavors. I'm not casting aspersions either; such people are us, many of these people mean well and are doing the best they know how (often better than the rest of us), and I'm certainly not going to waste both our times sitting here and categorizing each individual person into the "true saint" or "fake saint" category. I'm not running a tally.

Objectively speaking, wherever the shoe fits: the saint of which I'm writing is someone who has a stomach and guts, as well as a perceptive mind cleared of all our unfortunate, typical detritus. The saint is a fully-actualized human being. Saints know how to laugh *and* cry, are happier than we limping sinners know how to handle, or angrier, or whatever else. Truth be told, encountering a saint is a terrifying experience. We don't shock or provoke any clutched pearls in the saint by talking irreverently about Virginia's white confirmation dress; we'll provoke in the saint a deep sorrow for us that threatens to bring us to our own sorrow over ourselves, and maybe (if we're getting a little too frisky) we'll provoke a verbal or physical rebuff that, at least afterward, we'll admit was justly administered with a horrifying and righteous anger.

Perhaps, Beloved, you're surprised by the notion of comparing a saint to the creepy man/boy (or man-boy?) cajoling a young girl and looking to get lucky. I suspect you've already connected the dots, but let's not take it for granted here. (I've already bloviated extensively in this letter several times; why not keep doing so?) Maybe a less cluttered comparison would be: saints are the artists who ride rockets, or the drug addicts who seek the fix – only they've figured and felt out how it's supposed to work in their human life in an ultimate and fully-integrated way. The artist and addict are human, but so are the saints. The saints have found and succumbed to ecstasy as it's truly meant to be experienced, moving outside of merely themselves and their own experience. They've "cracked" the "code" and found the rocket, the trip, that we're looking for in our rocket launches and drug trips and yet have been unable to find for ourselves in a sustainable way. They've become love. They've become all flame, to borrow words from a monk who was praying his life away happily in the desert.

Simon Tugwell, in his *Prayer: Living with God*, hit a certain nail on the head when he offered his commentary on the Parable of the Prodigal Son. I assume you've heard that story told, Beloved, as it's a classic, but (again and again) I'll summarize it here in case you haven't. Once upon a time, there was a man who had two sons. The younger son did the old-school equivalent of saying "I wish you were dead" to his father by demanding his own portion of the inheritance. This younger son proceeded to leave home and live a lavish lifestyle on that inheritance until a famine struck the region, and then (destitute) he found himself starving, working on a farm, and lusting after the slop the pigs received. One day, he came to his senses and asked himself: "Don't the servants in my father's house have more than enough to eat? Well, in that case, I'll go to my father and say: 'Father, I've sinned against heaven and against you, I'm not worthy to be called your son, so just take me on as one of your hired hands.'" The father, meanwhile, in a completely different frame of mind, was holding a vigil for the younger son's return. When he caught sight of his younger son arriving, he didn't even let the son finish his prepared apology before ordering a party to celebrate the reconciliation. The older brother had remained faithful to the father this whole time, by the way, and now in his manifested pride and resentful indignation he refused to enter the party for his younger brother's return. The father tried to reason with the older son. The end. (We're left wondering about the older son, and this was the original point of the parable.)

Tugwell's analysis could be paraphrased something like this. The older son doesn't know his father, nor the true richness of his father's love. The older son is the kind of "good" that we would describe in our little existential boat as "nice," a shadow-box saint; he is self-satisfied and lacks all hunger. I would go further still: the older son *seems* to lack all hunger, and that's part of my point in bringing up this story. When push comes to shove, *plenty* of appetite comes erupting to the surface in all the wrong ways. The older son embodies the "nice guy" nowadays who complains that no one will date him. In the aftermath of his father's merciful act, the older son stands (stomach and soul) outside the party and enters the story's dialogue by complaining about not getting what he's due for his faithfulness. The father has forgiven; the older son, ostensibly for the father's sake, stages a protest. The older son lingers in the limbo of reaction outside the party, with ambivalent and unacknowledged appetites. He remains (as Tugwell points out) self-condemned. He damns himself in his "goodness," in his "niceness." The father must come looking for him for there to be any hope of reconciliation and restoration, and even then we the readers are left with a cliff-hanger ending.

On the other hand, says Tugwell, the stomach of the younger son damns him but also ends up saving him. He insults his father and abandons the true riches he actually had (quite admirable in his wholeheartedness, if nothing else) in order to trade on ephemeral pleasures, but it's his same stomach – "don't the servants in my father's house have enough to eat?" – which begins the path to reconciliation with his father as well. In other words, the younger son is a person we can recognize: a person honest and authentic enough to have a stomach. This younger son doesn't leave the stomach behind. It's with him in the party at his father's house. The father's healing reconciliation has fully integrated the son's stomach into a new relationship worth living.

The saints have appetites just as you and I do, Beloved, and they haven't repressed them. All heroic virtue as self-repression – that's just a bit of popular fiction we tell ourselves in our little boat. The older son is the half-baked, incomplete portraiture of a saint, which we so often imagine as the real photograph of such people. The true saints have figured out what those appetites mean in an ultimate sense. They're the reformed younger son, burning and ready to deploy upon the father's party wherever it shows up, at a moment's notice. They've found themselves loved and received, have been reconciled and invested in, and so now have nothing to lose. The love of spouse, the love of family, the love of friend, the love of stranger – the saints have obtained it all, but they have obtained it by first obtaining the one love that aligns all of these other loves into something rich and true. They have found the one love that makes all their other loves hit their respective targets, until they're loving in ways that make them look to us like four-dimensional creatures dipping into our ongoing feudal tragedies.

When I sing of the love within and underneath all other loves, when I sing of the ultimate freedom discovered in commitment, it isn't a collection of abstract reveries to me, Beloved. I hold clearly in my heart and mind the beautiful face of Saint Therese alongside all our brothers and sisters who found the same way to fulfillment. Saint Therese experienced a love and a joy that received miracles and opportunities and consolations and was unabashed in the face of wracking pain, death, and even the enduring darkness of doubt itself. The desolation we flee became for her a source of consolation. Saint Therese possessed a strong will, found empowerment in her commitment, and lived all the other things which we hunger and thirst for and talk about among ourselves in half-sketched ways – and she did so in capable sacrifice, pouring herself out to her Beloved.

The clever, the dumb, the wasting, the conserving – everybody talks about the startling impact of the saints as though they were a different species than us. Or perhaps we prefer to lump these people somehow into the same category as that of the emotionally-constipated older son: the piety of the people we bump into who give us an aftertaste of an unenviable sainthood. How much more alarming that these people who are truly saints did and do exist among us, and that they aren't a species of animal different from us. Upon encountering what gets called their holiness, we see that it has a gritty realism to it. The saints had and have stomachs, like us, but in their giving well the gift of self out of true love they discovered what our innermost stomachs were made for. We try to insulate ourselves from them, pointing to them as "unique human beings" or speaking of them in neutered, condescending ways. It's far truer and more dangerous to admit that the saints are the true standard and that shits like me and most likely you are meant to be them, if only we were ever to allow ourselves to grow strong enough. We're the ones losing out on what they've found, not the other way around.

You have the capacity to be a saint, Beloved, as

do I. Yes, even you, and even me. I'm nowhere near that living ecstasy, and yet this love which you yourself have provoked within me is threatening to make a saint out of me yet.

Those Last Few Steps before We Reach Your Door Again

Here we are, floating together, in different social circles and circumstances, in the same little existential boat, with a lot of other people accompanying us. You and I inhabit different realms, but we (and many others with us) are in this common plight together. We know the architecture of the brain and psyche better than our ancestors did, and we know better how the body works than they did. We have a lot of great data, and we *do* have the general rule of "be nice" going for us. (That is, it's certainly better in most situations to be nice rather than to *not* be nice, if by "nice" we mean something approximating an affable kindness.) Never-before experienced self-expression and self-realization swim all around us, and in the midst of these great discoveries we find ourselves lonelier than ever and sadder than ever and feeling miserably misunderstood. We don't know how to love all the way, and often we don't love well even in the ways that we know we should.

(Again, Beloved, I'll say it a thousand times if it assists in clarity: I don't mean any of this as a lamentation of hopelessness or an angry diatribe aimed at humanity. I have plenty of sorrow as well as absolute and rippling anger, but it's not directed here at you nor whatever hasty effigy we could throw together. It's directed at the hatred directed at you.)

We hold some broken pieces, move forward,

and always discover something crucial within our-selves or within others that hasn't turned out quite how we needed it to turn out. Aren't we always hunting for some other supplement to the dilemma? Doesn't this always provoke the need for other remedies? Exhausted by possibility, we eventually concede on this battlefront or another that "nothing in life is perfect."

I wouldn't disagree with the notion that the good things we encounter in this life of ours tend always to be bittersweet and imperfect. The most important aspects of our lives bring elation and pain together; the most beautiful people and parts of our lives bring some suffering with them. Dissatisfaction can drive us toward better things between and among ourselves. What I call bullshit on is how modestly and efficiently we arrive at this conclusion every day, and with how small a territory we've become satiated.

It's like this. Imagine a man who discovers a beautiful valley. He builds a home by the river in the valley, plants his garden, and acquires some animals. He builds some fences around his garden to keep those lovable but mischievous animals where they need to be. He takes good care of his animals, and his animals appreciate him. He spends his days making repairs or weeding or helping some animal or another out of its distress. Other persons live nearby, others move into the valley, and they all share their lives together. The man is a good neighbor and grows in his down-to-earth love of his neighbors.

Now, this man recognizes his life isn't "perfect" in the sense of absolute ease or lack of frustration. Nothing in life worth the name "life" ever is, in this world. One of his neighbors routinely makes a nuisance out of himself, and it would be nice not to need to go rescue that one damn goat out of the briar patch every few days. And yet, when he weighs everything in the balance, he might very well get caught saying on certain days: "It's not a perfect life, but it's good."

Now imagine another man who has entered that same valley right at the edge, in a clearing. He doesn't bother building a house, because that idea doesn't occur to him or else he deems it too much work and far too grave a restriction for him. He describes himself (to himself) as a free spirit. He ventures toward the woods and finds wolves there, so now he lingers forever in the clearing, his back pressed against the safer hills. He gets rained upon and fends off the wolves from time to time and wonders why the wolves continue to pay him visits. He never hunts down the wolves, and he likes to consider the clearing his homestead. He collects bits of knowledge and fits them into his life where they will; the knowledge fits into his life and never the other way around. He thinks of his completely unencumbered, completely open-ended existence as the way any real person should live a life, as he goes about doing the same things over and over again, reinventing proverbial wheels and never inventing the actual wheel. He clings to his survival. He also never really finds the other persons in the valley, though he's happy to consider himself an expert on them, brushes against their lives from time to time. This man says quite often to himself, feigning satisfaction so fully that he no longer remembers that he's feigning it: "There's no such thing as a perfect life, so this is good enough."

I call bullshit on the second man's claim, because he threatens nothing except himself. What are your thoughts, Beloved? This man hasn't actualized nearly anything in his life. He hasn't really entered into the valley but tells himself that he has. He hasn't attempted to explore or build a house, nor has he even become a truly terrifying wild man (destroyer of wolves) or given himself over to rape and pillage. He has failed to really enter into the situation in which he finds himself, in any good or evil way. We could exercise some polite diplomacy on his behalf and label this loosely as a "lifestyle choice," but anyone being honest with themselves would admit to preferring the first man's situation to the second man's – if not for the fictional second man, at least for themselves. At least we artists would, wouldn't we, Beloved?

All the battles we fight – why do we fight them? Is it for anything that lasts for more than five minutes? Do we ever, within ourselves, love any of these people around us beyond the movements of emotion or utility? Do we even know what loving means or looks like? We find it more and more difficult to speak of it. All around us the propositions drone incessantly: be good, be nice, do noble things. Or: be yourself, be nice when you can, do noteworthy and rewarding things. And: balance is key. We follow an elaborate script that often contradicts itself. We regurgitate. We say these things to ourselves not because we necessarily believe them but because it's our turn to take up the creed at the dinner party. Surely it's better to be good, to be nice, to do noble things than to be evil, to be rude, to do villainous things. And meanwhile none of this even approaches the questions we must answer for our own good. We're feverishly busy with deferral.

Do we remember those times we've brushed up against a true love somewhere out there? What was it like for you, Beloved? What was it like to encounter such solidity in a world of ghosts? Have we ever willed the fulfillment of an enemy through our actions? Has this all-encompassing love ever informed our lives for any moment in or out of time until it drove us to speak and act with satisfying authenticity and consistency? What was that like? Do you remember, Beloved? Will we ever pay for true happiness with any of our actual skin, since it does come down to that?

The gifts we give must become the gift of ourselves. We must become gifts, simply. Even in my own case, Beloved, if I were to profess a love for you and then be uncharitable to my next-door neighbor, this would be a defect that needs healing. I wouldn't have expanded to my full capacity in such a case. I might, in fact, be living in my own dream world that doesn't correspond to reality. As it stands, my love for you has edified a gift already given, already there. As I sang earlier, the fullness of the gift could have been actualized in some other way but, for me, has been prepared to be actualized in this love I now hold for you.

The Proposal

I have dreaded this bit, not out of any doubt of what I've found and feel, nor out of any doubting of your intelligence or your feeling or your competence, but out of the bluntness of the proposal at long last and your probable familiarity with things so like it and so unlike it. Basically, I dread how ripe it all is for misunderstanding. I dread my stumbling in the attempt, and I dread what my own defects here might mean for your reception, the possibility of my messing this up for you. Now I will pull out a certain diamond ring from behind the bouquet of flowers, and there's a good chance you'll say: "Oh, so *this* has been what it's all about. In that case, no, thanks." I don't dread the rejection for myself. I have hope it will get through – hope beyond myself, it doesn't all rest on my shoulders – but my love for you makes me feel all the varying possibilities for the future here in the pit of my stomach. You can be sure of something and full of joy and still be wracked over sharing it, Beloved.

In a love letter even more than a marriage proposal, the timing is difficult to get right. It'd be easier for me to dodge the proposal itself and to simply leave all of what I've written so far, leave it standing on the page as though it were meant to be a high-sounding, self-involved, and merely philosophical work of some wayward navel-gazer. I could let you go back inside, walk away. Yet, this is the hour.

Am I going to beg to be spared from it now? This is the moment toward which I've been meaning to walk with you. This letter isn't a philosophical work, and all of that shit was simply the preface to walk with you and to hope to woo you. This is a love letter, and my love compels me to cross, at last, this final threshold and speak to you plainly.

My proposal could be two-pronged, for the sake of accommodating you. First, there's a palatable version of the proposal which I could float to you as a pretty-sounding and safe idea, which (because it's pretty-sounding and safe) you might be tempted to take up. It's commonplace and abstract enough as a proposal, because we all have an innate sense about its truth and therefore find it compelling. For all I know of you (again, not much), you're already busy about it in your life. Hell, you might already be geared up for the second prong of my proposal, for all I know, but I want to make sure my letter arrives to you, wherever you actually are.

(Now, Beloved, so far I haven't hidden any-thing from you, and so I won't start now: the fact is, I would only sing about the incomplete first option, because, if you were to take it up, your path might very well end up looking like mine and many other's and – sooner or later – suck you into the black hole singularity of the second proposal's joy and fulfill-ment. Your fullness of joy and fulfillment – that's what I'm trying to seduce you into, one way or an-other.)

Second, there's the unpalatable version that sounds like a lot of other noise which other people have made before, probably to you, perhaps not out of any actual love for you. *I* would do so out of love and out of love alone. And, because love for you has compelled every word of this letter, I'll lay out both versions of the proposal for you now.

The first version of the proposal:

You are a lovable person who is in fact (as we all know we are) a mixed bag. No doubt there's a lot that you doubt about yourself and regret in your life, but surely there's also a lot that's beautiful and a lot going well. You are lovable, and you can truly love. Hopefully you have already experienced this. And there's at least one person out here (me) who loves you, so there's that, too, for whatever it's worth.

Therefore, if you haven't already: recognize within yourself the gift of yourself, and that you were made to be a gift-receiver and gift-giver. Readily and generously accept the gifts of others. Be mindful of their gifts. When you go about doing anything, recognize that you are giving a gift that is meant to be part of the gift of yourself. Our emptying is how we're filled. Give generously and appropriately to grandparent, parent, sibling, friend, lover, acquaintance, puppy, and absolute stranger. Get better at this. While you're going about this, be present to the moments of your day. If you believe in a deity of some kind and the possibility of prayer, recognize your ability to pray for someone else when you're reminded of them. Do so, often. If you don't believe in a deity of some kind or the possibility of prayer, at least think warmly of the person and hold them close to you in your mind and heart. When you suffer something, suffer it well – with dignity and patience and acts of love – and offer it all up on someone else's behalf. Find the wellsprings of true love that are there, and make it a habit to drink of this on behalf of some person or another. If you get good at this sort of thing, your life will itself become love, in your love for whomever. You will make out of your life an habitual posture of love, and you'll become a participation itself in that love.

The pain threshold on that proposal doesn't make it impossible to embrace, right? Again, you might already be striving for this or succeeding at it. If so, good. If you stay true to this, you'll do yourself and the world a series of great favors.

The second version of the proposal:

The God who is the groundwork of all existence itself and perfect fulfillment itself is *agápē* – the Love that gives of itself, within itself, as the perfect Gift and the perfect Begifted. This God created everything we see out of love, and created us human beings in a representative "image" of this same Being, in order for us to enjoy and share that *agápē* whom God is, in a way analogous to the way God enjoys and shares.

At some point or another, as a species and in our own lives, we fucked it all up on a cosmic scale.

We, who subsist within Existence, decided we would set forth the terms of our own existence. This was always a possibility, unfortunately: we weren't intended for relational rape, and one can't share the depths of love as it is without allowing a beloved the means to say "no." We began calling what would destroy ourselves "good," at least in the moments before regret, and we began feeling that what this Love has made "good" was a terrifying restriction of our autonomy.

In a very slow (to us, in hindsight) and gradual reintroduction, God began wooing these strange creatures back to Himself in the midst of the mess, describing Himself as a marriage suitor. He was already intervening, but in the unrolling centuries (and according to our perception of things) He began ridiculously small and worked ridiculously slowly. All of us together – a rebellious spouse stewing in our shame and rebellion – needed the soft touch, and so God got to work with a small and steady scalpel (which nonetheless seemed like a ton of bricks to us). Superstitions and idols were the first cancerous mass to be addressed, and how we treated our fellow members of the tribe, and how we treated the stranger and those in need. It was all simple enough to propose and discern, and ever unfurling; we persisted in our rebellion in the main, of course, but this gradual work of His was preparing our hearts and leading up to something.

When the time was right, God showed up in-person to reveal Himself definitively. What He revealed as the definitive interpretation of Himself and of us was the revelation of Himself united to our human nature, given the name *Yeshua bar Yosef*, also of course known as Jesus of Nazareth. He didn't show us how to be nice but rather how to be human, which also does include being kind and good, being (what we would lately call) a saint. He taught us a lot of things, but the central parts were: it's time to quit your self-destructive behavior, I'm your way out of this mess, I'm redeeming the human race, I'm setting up a new way of living, follow me and learn my craft. His death on one of the worst means of execution shows us the depths of Platonic Love. The God who holds us in existence and who could allow us to vanish in a moment's lapse of thought or love, committed to us and chose us over Himself. The God of Existence-itself dignified us as worthy of love, when all we offered Him was the same hateful response we always had.

He said, essentially: "I want our relationship to be restored such that I have restored it in this human male you can hear and see and touch, this Jesus. But this man is also me, I am he, and all you have managed to return for my love is the rejection you've always given me. So be it. Even so, I do love you and forgive you. I still love you, all the way to the final breath. I have taken your body to myself so that I can offer you a love that goes all the way through a final breath. This is how omnipotent I am: that I can and will endure the worst you offer. I want there to be no more misunderstanding between us, and so I'll paint it in bright red letters. Here's how much I love you: I'll accept your bad gift and give it back to you, transformed, as the means of your redemption. I, who am innocent, will absorb what your guilt gives, because I'm strong and perfect enough to do so. I'll take the things you fear most – death and suffering – and receive into myself your bad gifts for what they are, I who am Existence itself, turning these into the weapons I use to conquer your own self-destruction. Maybe this will awaken within you the love that will save you, the love I have put there and for which I created you, the love that I am."

Of course, you probably know the rest of the song at this point, might have guessed it earlier along our way together here. This Jesus entered a life beyond the death we know – a life fascinating but of course mysterious to us who linger on this side of things – and He commissioned His ragtag collection of mystified and reformed deniers, doubters, and general incompetents (along with a few faithful women) to embody Him in the world and carry Him out to the world at large, on a mission to bring joyful captives back into restored communion with Him and each other.

So: you, an earthy creature with your own flaws and wounds, still bear that divine image within your very being. You are lovable, and I love you. Lest you get too discouraged by how generic this affirmation has all turned out – another preacher on a familiar street corner – I love you not only because God loves you, but because I saw *you* through and past your depiction of yourself in that one video, secondhand as it was and merely mediated. Both affirmations are true. I don't need anyone to enforce a doctrine to follow regarding you, because I've glimpsed only a hint of you (the part you were trying to hide, no less) and fallen in love with you! How messy and horrifying and ridiculous a person you no doubt are, but also (even from what little I glimpsed of you) how brilliant and beautiful and wonderful you must be in this world right now, breathing at the same time as me some part of this thin little atmosphere we both inhabit! You and I are breathing at this same moment, and I think of you with love and care.

Therefore: get yourself a copy of the *Catechism of the Catholic Church* or something like it. Read it, or (better yet) go to the back and look up topics of question, doubt, anger, or interest and read them. Father Mike Schmitz has a podcast ("The Catechism in a Year") which makes it all easier. Bishop Robert Barron also has his "Catholicism" series which presents all of it well enough.

At the same time, get yourself to a Catholic parish for Mass, wherever you happen to be. Pray at the Mass and watch and listen. Don't receive Communion yet; save that for later, for the special occasion I'm about to mention. Meet people as best you can, given your celebrity. I don't know how to navigate that one for you, I'm sorry to say. You seem clever enough; you'll figure this out. I have faith you'll find some pious and benevolently crazy old lady or a woman your age who intrigues and mystifies you, and the fact is that you'll eventually need other people like this (or even unlike it) to begin experiencing the Mystical Body in earnest.

Also: Move through, as best you can, any stupidity and self-inflicted wounds you encounter among us. Absorb it all for what it is – I'm not telling you to turn a blind eye to human faults or to play pretend with yourself – but let it become a part of a *whole* experience. In Western culture especially, we Catholics aren't doing so very well with this "becoming all flame" notion right now, if we ever have; we're all in various stages of recovery, and a lot of our mess is begging for drastic intervention. There are the people who know and practice nothing but call themselves Catholic, and the people who know and practice everything but haven't bothered to see the forest for all their favorite trees, and all sorts of other absurd conduct. Frankly, Beloved, it's a shit show these days, and in some way or another it always has been. Don't be distracted by the spiritual hospital beds and crazy people we have lying around everywhere. I'm in a bed over here somewhere, and there's one for you.

So, sure, notice all of this fuckery, poke any wounds you must and ask questions, and meanwhile get a meeting on the calendar with a priest or a deacon. Sniff them out. See if they seem to know what's going on. Ask the hardest questions. If they can't answer, find some other person – like that mystical woman your age or some other, more intimidating priest – who can. Enter into private instruction (someone teaching you the Catholic Faith) or, if you like your odds being around other people in a classroom setting, enter what's called OCIA (the parish office staff can help you navigate this). Receive Baptism, if you haven't already. Receive Confirmation, with or without Virginia's white dress. Receive Communion, and get to Confession when you've fucked it all up again. Try again and keep trying.

Ultimately: learn through all of this – despite all our and your laughable and ridiculous tragedies – that exactly *here* is where you'll find the Love you've already been seeking throughout your entire life, Who will ignite your own heart in full actuality with His love-beyond-all-loves. He will forge you into the fullness of the amazing creature you already are and were made to be. You will embrace any or all this poorly at first; we all do. Scant few of us get it right in the first attempt. But if you enter into this seeming-death well, you can and will become all flame, as the dehydrated monk put it – an all-consuming, undying, and terrifyingly beautiful bonfire. You will find a joy and a peace and a love that transcends all the aloofness and callous misunderstandings and insults and betrayals offered all around us. You will *know* Love and His acceptance like a spouse knows the habits of her beloved: this fire will *broil* within your own heart. You will find yourself dying with love and, in that active death, finding true life. You will find the life that can't be defeated or quenched even by the worst that has ever been offered, a love drawing all things into its furnace of fulfillment.

Please know that I have made exactly *none* of this second version of the proposal out of any crass and impersonal desire to "bag" you for "my" religion. It would break my heart if you thought so little of me, after all my ridiculous but well-meant prefaces and hedged explanations. Do you see my heart yet, Beloved? Draw a little closer in spirit, even now. Do you feel the heat of my own furnace yet? A preacher on the street would tell you that you're deprived of this and that and so on. Yes, I think you are, in all truth, or I wouldn't be writing to you. However, I will tell you even more vehemently: *we* are deprived of *you*. And *I* am deprived of you, mystically speaking. You are flesh of my flesh and bone of my bone, and so how can I not experience a share in sorrow so long as you aren't fully a part of this *Magnum Mysterium* that holds the world (and me) together?

Beloved, how is it possible that you and I could remain apart, on either side of this mystical joy's fullness? How can I rest on any laurels or relax in this battle of life, knowing that you aren't fully in communion with me in this Mystical Body nor fully fighting alongside me somewhere in the world? How could I have avoided writing a ponderous love letter, knowing that *I'm* not fully in communion with *you*, that (for all that is no doubt going right within your life) you remain apart? We are losing out on each other!

Beloved, I would give up every single grace and consolation that I have *ever* received if it could *all* be transferred to you somehow, to *you*. If your heart were to rejoice so fully that it became a sun of love in the sky for all to see and love and embrace, and the cost for that were my being forgotten by my closest friends in a dark cupboard somewhere, I would gladly choose it. If I could be damned for eternity so that you could experience a sliver of what a shit like me has experienced in the Sacrament of Confession, so that you could fall short of being a saint in this present life but arrive there some mystical day, I would accept that transfer at this very moment. Of course, this is all foolish talk – God doesn't want either of us to damn ourselves, I shouldn't want to be damned, and your own choices are yours to make – but, for my part, if that offer were ever on the table, I would embrace it with all my heart. This isn't hypothetical. Beloved, in moments of my more fevered joy, in the foolish mutterings of love, I have prayed such things.

What more can I write to you, Beloved? Letters – especially letters trying to express love – can only go so far. Mine has fallen terribly short of the mark, I'm afraid; the dead letter will never express the heart completely. Please do always know, wherever and whenever you are reading this, whatever you choose, whatever you don't choose, that I will always love you and will always be carrying an everlasting prayer for you in my heart. You are lovable and in fact loved. On your darker days, remember that at least one person in this world wants you to find your fulfillment and joy. Even if none of this makes any sense to you, even if you doubt me or my intentions, please do know of this immortal love, laugh me off and yet carry with you whatever encouragement it brings. Beloved, I will be offering up every triumph I can for you as a prayer and every suffering. I won't pretend that I'll content myself with being healed into a raging fire along this path if you won't be joining me, mystically, but for your sake I'll keep throwing lumber onto this fire of mine, offering up whatever I can, and hoping in the Source of all hope.

I will always remain Truly Yours, despite the blasphemous necessity of a pseudonym here for both our sakes,

"Bezalel"

Made in the USA
Columbia, SC
24 May 2024